INFP: Understanding & Relating with the Healer

MBTI Personality Types Series

By: Clayton Geoffreys

Copyright © 2015 by Clayton Geoffreys

All rights reserved. Neither this book nor any portion thereof may be reproduced or used in any manner whatsoever without the express written permission. Published in the United States of America.

Visit my website at www.claytongeoffreys.com

Cover photo by Israel Defense Forces is licensed under CC BY 2.0 / modified from original

Table of Contents

Foreword 1

An Introduction to MBTI 4

The Four Dimensions of the MBTI 7

Why is the Myers-Briggs Type Indicator Significant? 11

Uncovering the "Healers": Who is an INFP? 14

Why are INFPs Indispensable Leaders? 19

The 7 Greatest Strengths of an INFP 22

    1. Idealism 22

    2. Creativity 23

    3. Empathy and Compassion 23

    4. Belief in Equality 24

    5. Insightful 25

    6. Depth and Intelligence 26

    7. Loyalty and Dedication 26

The 5 Greatest Areas of Improvement for an INFP 28

    1. Extreme Idealism 28

  2. Extreme Selflessness 29

  3. Sensitivity to Criticism...30

  4. Tendency to Blame Oneself 31

  5. Prone to Distractions 32

What Makes an INFP Happy? 33

What are Some Common Careers of an INFP? 36

Common Workplace Behaviors of an INFP 40

  INFPs as Employees...41

  INFPs as Colleagues...42

  INFPs as Supervisors..43

INFP: Parenting Style and Values 45

Why Do INFPs Make Good Friends? 49

INFP Romance 52

  Best Personality Matches for INFPs 54

  Weaknesses 55

  Strengths 56

7 Actionable Steps for Overcoming Your Weaknesses as an INFP 59

    1. Learn to Plan Ahead 59

    2. Understand That No One is Perfect 60

    3. Set Incentives for Meeting Requirements ... 60

    4. Don't Be So Hard on Yourself 61

    5. Don't Take Things Too Personally 62

    6. Put Yourself First 62

    7. Be More Assertive 63

The 10 Most Influential INFPs We Can Learn From 64

    1. Antoine de Saint-Exupery 64

    2. Bill Watterson 65

    3. J.R.R. Tolkien 65

    4. Edgar Allan Poe 66

    5. Vincent van Gogh 66

    6. Hans Christian Andersen 67

    7. William Shakespeare 67

8. George R.R. Martin 68

9. Tim Burton 68

10. Johnny Depp 69

Conclusion 70

Final Word/About the Author 72

Foreword

Have you ever been curious about why you behave certain ways? Well I know I have always pondered this question. When I first learned about psychology in high school, I immediately was hooked. Learning about the inner workings of the human mind fascinated me. Human beings are some of the most impressive species to ever walk on this earth. Over the years, one thing I've learned from my life experiences is that having a high degree of self-awareness is critical to get to where you want to go in life and to achieve what you want to accomplish. A person who is not self-aware is a person who lives life blindly, accepting what some label as fate. I began intensely studying psychology to better understand myself, and through my journey, I discovered the Myers Brigg Type Indicator (MBTI), a popular personality test that distinguishes between sixteen types of individuals. I hope to cover some of the most prevalent personality

An Introduction to MBTI

You may have noticed that some people are naturally organized and systematic, while others can manage just fine without planning ahead. You may have wondered why some people prefer working alone, while others enjoy being part of a team. These are just a few things that can be explained by assessing someone's personality.

The Myers-Briggs Type Indicator (MBTI) test is an assessment designed to do just that. The MBTI posits that all your actions and decisions are inextricably tied to your innate tendencies. Even the seemingly random choices that you make are not random at all, but are rooted in the natural tendencies associated with your personality type. Why did you walk away during that confrontation? Why did you sign up to volunteer for that fundraiser? Why do you feel more comfortable alone? All these things can be explained by your personality.

The MBTI test was first published in 1962, by Katharine Cook Briggs and Isabel Briggs-Myers. The mother-daughter team originally devised the assessment to help women determine which jobs would be the most suitable for them. The idea came to them after studying the typological theories of Carl Jung. According to Jung, there are four main functions that people use to make decisions. Briggs and Myers took it further and began developing the MBTI to gauge people's cognitive preferences. Since then, the MBTI test has grown to become one of the most popular and highly-trusted personality evaluations in existence.

The MBTI questionnaire asks a series of questions that target the four primary dimensions of an individual's personality. Each dimension is made up of two opposing functions: extroversion vs. introversion, intuition vs. sensing, perceiving vs. judging, and thinking vs. feeling. While it can be argued that both qualities can manifest in a single person, the test shows which function is more dominant. For instance, you may possess both judging and perceiving traits, but judging is your more dominant function.

Your results in each dimension are combined to form a four-letter acronym which refers to your personality type. There are sixteen possible results. The sixteen types are then classified according to temperament. ESFP, ESTP, ISTP, and ISFP are classified as Artisans. ENFJ, INFP, INFJ, and ENFP are classified as Idealists. ISFJ, ISTJ, ESFJ, and ESTJ make up the Guardians. Finally, INTP, ENTJ, INTJ, and ENTP comprise the Rationals.

The Four Dimensions of the MBTI

Have you ever wondered why you see the world the way that you do? Have you ever thought about why you enjoy certain activities more than others? It all boils down to how you scored in each dimension of the Myers–Briggs Type Indicator (MBTI) test.

The MBTI explains that your personality can be divided into four separate dimensions. Each dimension represents a different function: how you interact with others, how you gather data from your surroundings, how you make choices, and how you perceive the world.

The four dimensions are:

1. Introversion (I) vs. Extroversion (E)

The first dimension refers to your energy levels when it comes to social interactions. Extroverts are energized by social interactions. If you are an extrovert, you feel most comfortable when you find yourself surrounded by other people. You find long periods of solitude exhausting. To recharge, you need to immerse yourself in the company of others. On the other hand, introverts are energized during moments of privacy and isolation. If introversion is your dominant function, you become drained after extended stretches of being around other people. It is not that you dislike social interaction; it is just that you value the quality of your interactions more than the volume.

2. Intuition (N) vs. Sensing (S)

This dimension is all about how you gather information from your surroundings. If your dominant function is sensing, you are most likely a critical thinker. You trust only what you can process using your five physical senses. You do not like making assumptions when there is no immediate proof to back it up. This makes you more practical and logical. Conversely, if your dominant side is intuition, you have the ability to read between the lines. You do not need facts when you have your gut feelings to rely on. Your thinking leans toward the abstract, and you have no problems seeing the bigger picture. You are future-focused, and you embrace possibilities.

3. Feeling (F) vs. Thinking (T)

The third dimension refers to the method by which you arrive at decisions. If you lean toward feeling, that means you use your emotions when making decisions. You follow your heart and can be very sympathetic toward other people. However, you also have the tendency to be illogical and highly sensitive. Thinkers, on the other hand, are more objective decision-makers. If you are a thinker, you are able to distance yourself from an emotional situation before making a choice. This does not mean you are cold and heartless; it only means you have the ability to take emotions out of the equation for the time being to arrive at a logical solution.

4. Perceiving (P) vs. Judging (J)

This dimension is all about how you perceive the outside world. If your dominant side is perceiving, that means you have a more carefree and laid-back attitude toward life. You do not like being tied down, and you value your freedom. You do not like making plans, because you want your life to be spontaneous. Routine and monotonous tasks bore you. If you are a judger, on the other hand, you prefer a life of structure and order. Planning is not a chore, but rather something you enjoy doing. You like having a clear schedule to follow. While this does make your life a bit predictable, it also makes you extremely reliable and committed. This also means that you value closure. You are unable to move on from something unless it has been seen to completion.

Why is the Myers-Briggs Type Indicator Significant?

In this day and age, most people work toward the goal of personal fulfillment. Self-awareness and an understanding of oneself have become valued assets. For that, and a variety of other reasons, the Myers-Briggs test has grown to become an essential tool in achieving success.

Identifying your personality type can help you gauge the strengths and weaknesses that are unique to your type, which will then enable you to improve and overcome them. Understanding your motivations and natural tendencies can be useful in many practical applications, such as career selection and other major life decisions. It can also provide you with the self-awareness required for personal development and success.

Furthermore, the MBTI gives you useful insight into the minds of other people. By knowing what makes people tick, you can create healthier and more harmonious interpersonal relationships. It can help you understand why people make certain choices when confronted with a particular situation. It can also teach you how to communicate more effectively with others. It can open the door toward more productive working environments and more successful social interactions. This is especially helpful when it comes to friendships and romantic relationships. Does your best friend get upset when you do not reply to their messages right away? Does your significant other ignore you during fights? Do they come across as controlling at times? These are only a few of the things that can be explained by understanding their personality type.

The MBTI test also has numerous uses in other fields, such as in the workplace and at school. It can help you identify the tasks and activities you excel in and enjoy.

Do you prefer working alone or as part of a team? Can you focus on more than one thing at a time? Are friendships important to you in the workplace? Chances are, it has something to do with your personality. By knowing your type, you can make career-related decisions that will be most beneficial to you in the long run. If you are still in school, it can help you make choices that are more aligned to your natural inclinations.

Overall, the MBTI test is an essential tool in achieving success in the workplace and in your personal life.

Uncovering the "Healers": Who is an INFP?

INFP is one of the personality types according to the Myers-Briggs Type Indicator (MBTI). The acronym stands for Introversion Intuition Feeling Perceiving. One of the rarer personality types, INFPs make up only 4% of the general population.

The cognitive functions of INFPs are as follow:

- Dominant: Introverted Feeling (Fi) - Your dominant function refers to the role you feel most comfortable portraying. As an INFP, your dominant function is Introverted Feeling. This means you process information based on abstract ideas and deeply-embedded values. It also means you possess a natural feel for what does, and does not, belong.

- Auxiliary: Introverted Intuition (Ne) - Your auxiliary function serves to expand your dominant function. In INFPs, the auxiliary function is Introverted Intuition, which allows you to delve into hidden possibilities. You are skilled at seeing the larger picture, and you relate to the world by mainly using your intuition.

- Tertiary: Introverted Sensing (Si) - Your tertiary function is less developed than your dominant and auxiliary functions. However, there is a large possibility that it will become more pronounced over time. As an INFP, your tertiary function is Introverted Sensing, which refers to collecting information and assessing how it relates to past experiences.

- Inferior: Extroverted Thinking (Te) - Your inferior function can also be called your Achilles' heel. It refers to the role you are least comfortable fulfilling. If you are an INFP, Extroverted Thinking is your inferior function. This means you are uncomfortable with restrictions and strict schedules.

As an INFP, you are a genuine idealist. You believe that every person has some good in them, and you look at the bright side of any situation. Initially, you might be described as quiet and shy, but you are actually a passionate and fun-loving person. Furthermore, you are guided by your own set of values and beliefs, rather than logic. Since your personality type is so uncommon, there is a high chance that you might be misunderstood by some people. However, those who take the time to get to know you value your caring and compassionate nature.

INFPs are also known as Healers. It is common for Healers to be perceived by others as reserved and distant. Inside, however, you possess a capacity for caring that is not seen in other personality types. As the term implies, one of your main goals is to heal the inner conflicts of the people you care about. You also strive to bring harmony to the organizations and causes you believe in.

As a Healer, you possess a rare idealism that stems from your strong personal values. You believe that the world is a good place, filled with so many wonderful possibilities. You are guided by a deep sense of morality and virtue, rather than the promise of rewards and recognition.

INFPs are good communicators, although you often use metaphors and symbols to get your message across. You are gifted at self-expression, and you reveal your deepest thoughts and emotions through creative methods. For that reason, it is not unusual for many INFPs to become writers, poets, and artists.

As an INFP, you enjoy losing yourself in your imagination. You can spend hours in deep thought, contemplating the theoretical. In your mind, there are hundreds of possibilities forming each minute. This can sometimes cause you to lose touch with the real world, and make you neglect your personal needs. This is why other people sometimes see INFPs as disorganized and scatter-brained.

Although you are moved by your desire to heal and help people, you choose to focus on a few people or a single cause at a time. Because of your introverted roots and inclination toward perception, taking on too many things at once can be too exhausting and draining for you. Furthermore, you can sometimes become overwhelmed when faced with all the negative things in the world that you cannot fix.

Why are INFPs Indispensable Leaders?

INFPs, in general, are reluctant leaders. This is mainly because INFPs are carefree and laid-back people who are uncomfortable with hard guidelines and strict schedules. As an INFP, you would much rather play the supportive role and cooperative follower than an authoritative leader. You have no desire to exercise control over the people around you. This does not mean you do not have what it takes to become an effective leader. You just prefer not to be in the spotlight. That said, when you are faced with a cause you personally believe in, you have no problem taking charge.

As an INFP, your leadership style can be described as passionate and encouraging. You make sure that all the members of your team are given equal opportunities to shine. You strive toward a harmonious working environment, and for that reason, you are quick to address any concerns your team members might have.

Because of your intuition and sensitivity, you can sense whenever there are unspoken issues that need to be taken care of.

As a leader, you have a strong sense of what is right and wrong, and your strong beliefs have the tendency to rub off on other people. You are able to inspire and motivate your employees through your positive energy and supportive nature. You approach leadership with gentle determination. You are also an excellent listener, and you are adept at pushing others to use their gifts and potential. Your quiet and reserved demeanor allows you to lead without being seen as domineering or overbearing.

When it comes to accomplishing goals, you have a big-picture approach. You have no problem taking on a project even when a clear plan has not been laid out. In fact, you would much rather adapt to the circumstances as you go along. Your lack of planning does not mean you are all over the place. It is quite the opposite, in fact. You are actually a perfectionist, and you demand the best from your team. That said, you encourage your team members to think creatively. You invite each of them to provide input and suggestions, so that you can collectively come up with a course of action.

It is also interesting to note that, among the personality types, you are least likely to "look" like a manager. In fact, your desire for equality leads you to do away with the typical boss-subordinate dynamic. You prefer to treat other people as equals, and you want them to treat you the same way. However, this quality also makes you uncomfortable with providing feedback. You do not want to hurt other people's feelings, so you shy away from giving them constructive criticism that will benefit them in the long run.

The 7 Greatest Strengths of an INFP

As an INFP, you possess various strengths that are unique to your personality type. Identifying these natural strengths will provide you with the opportunity to improve them even further, making it easier for you to find your purpose and place in the world.

1. Idealism

Rainbows after the rain, clouds with silver linings – these sayings must have been written by an INFP. Unlike any other personality type, you possess a sense of idealism that is both honest and pure. You genuinely believe in the good of mankind and that the world is a kind and loving place. You are extremely optimistic, and whenever possible, you choose to look at the bright side of any situation. Because of this belief, you are remarkably strong when faced with challenges.

2. Creativity

As an INFP, you possess a creative mind and, more importantly, the skill to express your creativity. When this gift is given the opportunity to flourish, you can create inspiring works of art. In fact, many INFPs are poets, authors, and artists. Be it through writing, painting, drawing, or photography, you turn to art for self-expression. However, you do not need to be recognized for your work. On the contrary, the mere act of creating something beautiful is enough to make you genuinely happy. Furthermore, you tend to see things differently from other people, and your unique perspective is especially evident in the art you create, regardless of the medium you find yourself using.

3. Empathy and Compassion

INFPs are highly sensitive. It is natural for you to empathize with other people's emotions and troubles. In fact, you are highly aware of the various forms of injustice that people suffer in our society. For that reason, you are extremely compassionate toward the less-privileged and disadvantaged members of your community. It is not uncommon for you to look for ways to help them. This may be through volunteering to help the poor, assisting the elderly, or helping those with special needs. You derive personal satisfaction from helping people in ways that will provide practical benefits for those in need. Your empathy and compassion do not only apply to injustice on a large scale, but also to the problems your friends and loved ones face on a regular basis.

4. Belief in Equality

You have a strong sense of justice, and you believe that all people should be treated equally. As a result, you are highly respectful of other people's opinions and beliefs, as long as your own values are not attacked or criticized. You have a "live and let live" approach toward life, and you believe that people should have the freedom to live their lives whichever way they choose, regardless of society's standards. In your mind, no one should be discriminated against because of who they are. In fact, you find diversity beautiful. In fact, the people who are closest to you admire your tolerant and accepting nature. When given the chance, you can become a source of comfort and healing for those who have been discriminated against in the past.

5. Insightful

As an INFP, you possess the ability to read other people. Even though you are an introvert, your sensitivity and intuition allow you to immediately understand a person's motivations, making it easy for you to relate to them. Due to this, you have deep insight into other people's personalities. This quality makes you suited for professions such as counseling or psychology. INFP writers will also benefit from this, since it can enable them to create realistic and profound characters.

6. Depth and Intelligence

INFPs are usually profound and intelligent. As a result, you can understand difficult and complicated concepts with relative ease. Learning new things are easy for you as well. However, you rarely find satisfaction in utilizing your intelligence, unless you are doing something that holds personal significance for you. You do not view success the same way that others do, so even though your intelligence and quick thinking can help you achieve conventional success and recognition, you would much rather put your abilities to use doing things that matter to you on a personal level.

7. Loyalty and Dedication

You are extremely loyal and dedicated. Since you value your privacy and solitude, you may be hard to get to know. However, those who are close to you know how loyal and dedicated you are. You are fiercely protective of those you care about, and you are always willing to stand up and defend your friends and family when they are wronged. Your loyalty not only applies to the people you love, but also to the causes you believe in. You take your beliefs very seriously, and you will fight for them at all costs. If you are part of an organization that shares your values and goals, you will dedicate your time and resources to help that organization.

The 5 Greatest Areas of Improvement for an INFP

As an INFP, you possess a number of remarkable characteristics. However, there are also some aspects of your personality that need to be worked on. Understand that although these qualities are natural traits of an INFP, it is possible to improve and overcome them. By identifying and understanding these areas of improvement, you are well on your way toward personal growth and success. An interesting thing to note is that these qualities are, to a certain extent, related to your greatest strengths.

1. Extreme Idealism

Although your idealism can be an admirable quality, taking it too far can work against you. There are times when your idealism can set you up for failure and become a source of disappointment and sadness. One example of this is if you make it your personal mission to make the world a kinder place. In spite of your good intentions, bad things will continue to happen, which will inevitably disappoint you. This is also true when it comes to your personal relationships. You tend to have highly idealized views of the people you love. In your eyes, they can and should do no wrong. Unfortunately, no one is perfect, and sooner or later, they will make mistakes. It is important for you to remember that people are fallible beings who will inevitably make mistakes.

2. Extreme Selflessness

As a Healer, your primary goal is to fix people's problems and ease their troubles. You will do everything in your power to help them. The truth of the matter is there is only so much that you can do, and you hate the idea of not being able to help everyone. In fact, in spite of your selflessness, there are times when you see yourself as selfish, simply because there is so much more that you wish you could do. This belief causes you to push even harder, often forgoing your own needs and well-being just to be able to help other people. If this goes on, you might end up sacrificing your own health and happiness. Remember, you have to help yourself before you can help anyone else.

3. Sensitivity to Criticism

As an INFP, you tend to take criticism quite personally. Whenever you are given negative feedback about a task or an activity, you feel as though your entire self is being criticized. You often forget that feedback is meant to be taken objectively and is provided as an opportunity to push yourself to do even better. There are times when criticism can sound like a personal attack against you. There are even instances where you perceive criticism, even when none is intended. This can cause you to react emotionally, or even to shut down completely. When faced with criticism or constructive feedback, it is important for you to remember that they are not criticizing you as a person. It only means that you can do better in relation to that particular task or activity.

4. Tendency to Blame Oneself

You possess the tendency to blame yourself when something does not go as expected. Even if it is something that you could not have possibly controlled, you end up thinking that it is your fault. Such thoughts can cause you to develop a low self-esteem, and later on, you might end up being too critical of yourself and your actions. This is also why you can be such a perfectionist sometimes. When something goes wrong, you feel like it is your fault, so you try to do things as perfectly as you can the first time around. This is also related to your desire to heal. You make it your personal mission to fix everyone else's problems because failing to do so weighs heavily on your shoulders. You begin thinking that you are personally responsible for their troubles. INFPs who notice this quality in themselves should remember to ease up.

Take it easy on yourself. You cannot control everything. There are some things that are just out of our hands.

5. Prone to Distractions

Because of your inclination toward perceiving, you might find it difficult to see things through to completion. You have the tendency to leave a project unfinished when something else comes along that piques your interest. Furthermore, you have a very active imagination. It is common for your mind to drift while in the middle of performing a task. Because of this, it can sometimes be hard for you to focus on the task at hand, especially if it is something you do not personally believe in.

What Makes an INFP Happy?

INFPs are called Healers for a reason. Whether it is adopting a pet from the local pound or volunteering at a homeless shelter, nothing makes you happier than helping those in need. You love being a source of comfort for others, and you are always eager to lend a helping hand.

Due to your introverted roots, privacy and personal space are very important to you. Furthermore, you enjoy spending time alone and letting your imagination run free. Other personality types might find it odd, but you are genuinely happy making up stories in your head and thinking about abstract ideas and possibilities. For that reason, you value people who respect your need for solitude.

You can be quite difficult to get to know. It takes a while before you start opening up, and there are only a handful of people you feel genuinely close to.

However, those people mean the world to you. Their happiness is tied to your happiness. You will do everything in your power to ensure that their needs are fulfilled. Knowing that they are happy and taken care of provides you with a profound sense of personal satisfaction. However, you also want your actions to be appreciated. You are happiest when you feel valued. Verbal affirmation means a lot to you. Without it, you can feel neglected and undervalued.

As an INFP, you are constantly searching for meaning in your life. You need a sense of purpose and a source of inspiration. Because of this, you seek out experiences and people that ignite intense emotions in you. This also applies to romantic relationships. In fact, you tend to get bored and restless when the intensity and passion begin to wane.

Another thing that makes you happy is art; creating art, to be more specific. You have a gift for communicating through symbols and metaphors. As such, you are drawn to poetry, books, and other art forms. You use art as a means of self-expression. In fact, you do not require recognition for your work. The mere act of expressing yourself in an artistic way is enough to make you happy.

Your inclination toward perceiving means that you are happiest when you feel free and unencumbered. In contrast, you tend to shut down in situations where you feel cornered and smothered. Routines and schedules make you feel trapped. You would much rather live life untethered where you are free to do as you please.

What are Some Common Careers of an INFP?

Career selection is an important life decision that can affect not only your own life, but the lives of others as well. For that reason, choosing a career path should be done with care. It is important to consider the fact that certain careers are more aligned with the natural characteristics of certain personality types. For example, would a reserved introvert be happy in a workplace where social interactions played a huge part? Probably not. Sure, they might be able to get the job done, but they would leave work feeling exhausted and stressed out.

As an INFP, there are many aspects of your personality that you should consider when selecting a career path. You are a compassionate egalitarian with a strong sense of right and wrong. You value your personal space and freedom, and you will most likely find satisfaction in careers that enable you to utilize your intelligence and creativity. You want a job that lets you do something you believe in – something that allows you to contribute to the betterment of other people's lives. It is especially important for an INFP to choose a career that coincides with your natural inclinations, because if not, you will end up feeling dissatisfied, restless, and generally unhappy.

You are likely to enjoy working for an organization that shares the same values and principles as you do. Organizations that are focused on helping people in real and tangible ways are a good fit. This is why many INFPs choose a career in health care. Ideal health care jobs for an introverted feeler include speech pathology, physical therapy, occupational therapy, and psychology. You will find these jobs appealing, because not only do they give you an avenue to help and heal others, they allow you to focus on one patient at a time.

Aside from health care, your compassion and desire to heal can also be used in fields that deal with helping people that are emotionally broken. Jobs such as social work and counseling are a few examples. These jobs also allow you to create more meaningful connections with the people that you are helping.

As an INFP, you have very developed language skills, which make it easy for you to learn new languages. INFPs who take the time to master a second or third language can pursue a career in translation or interpretation.

Your creative mind and artistic abilities are also things that have to be considered when selecting a career. You love creating and expressing your emotions and thoughts through metaphors, symbols, and other abstract ways. For this reason, you are likely to gain satisfaction from jobs that require creativity. Some examples are writing, fine arts, graphic design, and multimedia arts.

In general, someone with an inclination toward perceiving might not fare well in fast paced and highly pressurized working environments. You would much rather work in a place where you are given the opportunity and freedom to operate at your own pace. Jobs with a more laid-back and carefree atmosphere are ideal. This is why so many INFPs find satisfaction in doing freelance work. Not only does it give you the relaxed vibe that you seek, it also gives you room to pursue your other interests. If you are lucky, you would be able to find a job that merges these two together, such as freelance photography or freelance writing.

Common Workplace Behaviors of an INFP

As an INFP, it can be a challenge not to take your career personally. You believe that the work you do is a direct reflection of who you are. For this reason, it is almost impossible for you to work in an organization whose mission opposes your personal values and beliefs. You are most interested in jobs that are personally significant to you. In fact, if you find yourself doing a job just for the sake of doing it, you immediately lose interest and may even act rebelliously.

Because of your introverted nature, you prefer a workstation that lets you have privacy. Not only does this give you your own personal space, it also helps you shut out distractions that can keep you from focusing. You can sometimes be disorganized, simply because practicality is not important to you. It is not uncommon for your desk to be cluttered, because you do not find organization necessary to get your job done. However, if the task at hand can best be completed in an organized manner, you try your best to do so. In fact, you tend to be a perfectionist. Even when a task is technically completed, you might not see it as finished. There are always things that can be improved, edited, and revised. You simply have a hard time bringing a project to closure. Furthermore, you have pictured the finished project in your head so many times that the actual output becomes less important. The big picture is more significant to you.

INFPs as Employees

You are a creative thinker. As a result, you often come up with interesting perspectives that have been considered by other people. You are very adaptable, and you can easily think of new ways of doing things depending on the current situation. Sometimes though, you have trouble with meeting deadlines. You have the tendency to take on new tasks that interest you, thinking you still have a lot of time to get it done, which leads to procrastination and panicking as the deadline approaches.

Unlike other personality types, you do not need recognition for your contributions. Sure, you want to feel appreciated and acknowledged, but you have no desire to be in the spotlight. Competition does not interest you. Knowing that you have contributed to a project that helps someone improve their quality of life is more than enough for you. In fact, you prefer looking at your accomplishments based on the service you provide others, rather than from a business standpoint.

INFPs as Colleagues

Although you prefer working alone, you have no problem working alongside a team, provided that the rest of the members share the same vision as you. It bothers you to see your teammates working toward varying goals. Even so, it is highly unlikely that you will say anything about it. You do not like controlling other people, just as you do not like being controlled.

Your colleagues may describe you as friendly and laid-back. Even though you might emotionally distance yourself from the people you work with, you always make the effort to be polite and friendly. You dislike conflict, and you will do everything in your power to maintain an atmosphere that is warm and harmonious.

INFPs as Supervisors

As a leader, you are gentle, encouraging, and inclusive. You make sure that all members of your team are given equal opportunities to showcase their abilities. Your approach is more determined than aggressive. As a result, you would rather facilitate than direct. You invite your subordinates to come up with their own ideas and suggestions on how to get a project done. You would rather collectively come up with a group decision than bark out orders.

Overall, you thrive in a flexible environment where you can utilize your natural strengths to improve the lives of others.

INFP: Parenting Style and Values

As an INFP parent, you are deeply attuned to the needs and emotions of your children. For this reason, you are quick to provide them with their basic needs. This includes ensuring that they are warm and well fed. You are also quick to address their emotional needs. You are always there to provide them with hugs and words of encouragement. When your children come to you asking for advice, you are there to give them insight and support. Once you have given them advice, you are willing to let them go along and make their own decisions.

Children raised by INFP parents know, without a doubt, that they are loved and valued. They know that they have been taken care of, and they are comfortable in their knowledge that all their needs are going to be met. Furthermore, they learn at an early age how to show affection to the people they love. Because their emotional needs were always addressed, they learn to sense when someone else needs comforting. They also learn that they can approach their parents when they need support and encouragement.

From the very beginning, you derive immense joy from seeing your children explore, play, and discover the world. You are far from controlling. In fact, you allow your kids to experience things for themselves. You provide them with the freedom they need to make their own choices and learn things their own way. That said, you try to instill in them the same values and principles you believe in, hoping that those beliefs will guide them in the future. INFPs are idealists. This is also true when it comes to your children. You hold them to the same high standards that you hold yourself to. So when they fail to meet your expectations or they stray from the set of values that you have tried to instill in them, you may feel disappointment.

When your children decide to take on endeavors to further their intellect or artistic gifts, you are quick to support them. The same goes for your children's other interests such as sports and music. Aside from verbal encouragement, you also provide them with an environment where they can explore their gifts and talents, such as surrounding them with books, musical instruments, or art supplies.

Although you find it difficult to show your true self to other people, this can be an asset when it comes to parenting. This allows you to present yourself as a positive role model to your children, while shielding them with from your emotional outbursts. This also enables you to protect them from the cruelty of the world. Furthermore, you are able to provide them with a harmonious and conflict-free environment to grow up in.

One challenge an INFP faces as a parent is setting rules and routines. You dislike planning and making schedules and as a result, it can be hard for you to set boundaries and structure. For example, if your child breaks curfew, you might just let it slide, because your flexible nature makes it difficult to enforce rules and punishments. In fact, the only time when you will feel the need to discipline your children is when they do something that goes against your personal values and ideals.

Why Do INFPs Make Good Friends?

As an INFP, there are only a few people that you feel truly close to. Aside from the fact that you are naturally quiet and reserved, you are often misunderstood by some people because your personality type is so rare. That said, those that make the effort to get to know you can attest to your loyal and caring nature as a friend.

Truth be told, you are quite difficult to get to know. This can be a bit unfair to others, because you have such deep understanding of the personalities of other people, but you do not let others see the real you right away. As a result, most people you become close to are other NF types, because they are able to pick up on the little things that give them insight about who you are as a person. They are also the people who are most likely to be drawn to your enigmatic and mysterious aura.

Furthermore, you are not the type to make friends easily. You believe that friendship is something that has to be earned. With that said, the people who eventually earn your stamp of approval become lifelong friends who you deeply value and care about. When you begin caring about someone, your helpfulness and compassion shine through. You are always quick to help a friend in need, and because you are so intuitive, you are able to sense when someone is in pain, even if they do not say it outright.

By nature, you are a private person who values your personal space. As a result, you can become annoyed when you feel like your space is being invaded, especially by someone you are not close to. Furthermore, you value your alone time and privacy so much that there may be instances when you want to disappear for a little. This is not because you want to abandon your friends entirely. You just need to reconnect with yourself and spend some time recharging through solitude and reflection. In fact, you often come out of those moments feeling refreshed and renewed.

As mentioned previously, you are extremely uncomfortable with conflict. You want your friendships to be as smooth and harmonious as possible. Because of this, it is not uncommon for you to walk away, shut down, or act inappropriately during arguments and confrontations. An example of an inappropriate response to conflict is attempting to make light of the situation. This might cause your friends to think that you are not taking the situation seriously, but in reality, this is just your way of avoiding conflict.

INFP Romance

As an INFP, you usually hide your true personality underneath a calm and gentle exterior. Most people would be surprised to find out that you are actually an intense and passionate person who has a great capacity for love and affection.

INFPs are dreamers, and this quality is most apparent in your quest for the perfect relationship. In general, you have high expectations of the people you interact with, and it is doubly the case when it comes to romantic relationships. In fact, you do not just idealize your partner, you idolize them. You place them on a pedestal and expect them to live up to the ideal you have in your mind of what a perfect partner should be like. Of course, no one can live up to such expectations, and it is important for you to understand that relationships require compromise and understanding.

Because there are only a handful of people that you are truly close to, you embrace romantic relationships with a passionate intensity that is unique to your personality type. That said, you are not the type to jump head first into a relationship. In fact, you are quite wary of making long term commitments. Add that to your idealism, the initial stages of dating may involve comparing your current partner to the image of the ideal partner you have in your mind. However, as the relationship begins to grow, you become an encouraging and supportive partner who always puts your significant other's needs before your own.

As a partner, your empathy and sensitivity are heightened even more. You are able to intuit your partner's needs, and that enables you to address them in a timely manner. However, because you keep your emotions under the surface, your partner might not be able to read your needs and concerns, unless they are highly intuitive as well.

You allow your partner to be independent. You let them explore their own hobbies and interests, and you would like them to do the same for you. As a result, you are rarely seen as smothering. However, your ideals can sometimes lead you to offer them suggestions on how to improve their life or become better at their endeavors, which can cause your partner to feel like they are not good enough.

Best Personality Matches for INFPs

Although it can be argued that two people, regardless of personality type, can build a healthy and successful relationship, there are certain types that just seem to naturally work well together. In the case of INFPs, your best matches are ENFJs and ESFJs.

First of all, INFP-ENFJ and INFP-ESFJ matches work well because their extroverted nature can help pull you out of your shell. They can help you learn how to be more vocal about your opinions and emotions.

Furthermore, because you share an inclination toward feeling, you both tend to be more empathic and sensitive toward the needs of others. As someone who puts their partner's needs above their own, you need someone who will be able to intuit your needs right back, so that your health and well-being are also taken care of. Their judging sides will also work well with your perceiving side, because they will be able to provide you with much needed structure and order later on in life.

Weaknesses

Here are a few things you can work on for healthier romantic relationships:

- Too idealistic - You tend to put your partner on a pedestal. You have such high expectations of them, and it is impossible for them to live up to the image of the ideal partner that you have in your mind. It is important for you to understand that everyone has flaws and makes mistakes.

- Dislike Criticism and Conflict - You tend to take criticism rather personally. When that happens, you feel like your entire persona is under attack. This can cause you to react emotionally or walk away entirely. Because you dislike conflict so much, you would rather avoid confrontations and arguments.
- Difficulty Leaving an Unhealthy Relationship - The truth is most relationships are already over long before they actually end. However, you have a hard time seeing this. If you have invested so much of your time and energy into a relationship, you tend to blame yourself when things go bad. For that reason, you would rather stay and try to make it work, even if it is already time to end things.

Strengths

As an INFP, here are a few of your relationship strengths:

- Not Controlling - You prefer to live an untethered life, free and unencumbered from hard rules and restrictions. This is especially evident in your romantic relationships. You do not want to feel caged in or tied down, and you do not feel the need to control your partner. You let them pursue their own independent interests, and you do not nag them when they get home a bit late or if they are going out with their friends.
- Sensitive to Partner's Needs - You are highly intuitive, and you are able to read your partner's feelings. You can sense when they need something, and you are quick to provide that for them. You can also sense when something is bothering them; in which case, you are there to comfort and support them. You can tell when they are particularly happy or excited about something, and you make it a point to encourage and celebrate with them.

- Good Listener - You are genuinely interested in the events and happenings in your partner's life. Whether it is a major life event or just the mundane details of their day, you are happy to sit next to them on the couch and hear all about it.

7 Actionable Steps for Overcoming Your Weaknesses as an INFP

There is no sure tried and tested, step by step method to achieve success, but identifying your weaknesses and knowing how to overcome them is essential for personal development and potential greatness.

Here are seven actionable steps that can help you work through your weaknesses as an INFP.

1. Learn to Plan Ahead

Planning and making schedules are not things that you enjoy doing. They are, however, necessary to live a more successful life. With that in mind, you have to learn how to plan ahead. Start with the little things at first, until you become more comfortable with making long term plans and commitments. You can begin by calling up a friend to make dinner plans for the weekend. Easy, right? Then once you follow through on that, make plans ahead for the future. Book a romantic getaway for you and your significant other. Make plans to see a movie that is showing next month. Pretty soon, you will start to see that making plans is not so bad after all. In fact, it gives you something to look forward to and be excited about.

2. Understand That No One is Perfect

You have extremely high expectations of the people around you. You idealize them to the point that anything they do that is not aligned with the ideal you have set in your mind can disappoint you. Understand that the people you love are just that – people. They are human beings who make mistakes, and those mistakes do not make them any less beautiful or fascinating or remarkable.

3. Set Incentives for Meeting Requirements

You sometimes struggle with seeing things to completion. You often let your mind roam while doing certain tasks and this causes you to lose focus.

Sometimes, you abandon a project because something more interesting comes along. To overcome this, appreciate the benefits of sticking to your obligations. You can do this by giving yourself little rewards that you can only collect upon successful completion of the task.

4. Don't Be So Hard on Yourself

As a Healer with a high sense of idealism, you see it as your personal mission to heal the troubles of the world. Of course, there is only so much that you can do to help. There are times when failure to help someone can cause you to be overly critical of yourself. You may even begin to think that you are personally responsible for the hurt that they are feeling. Do not be too hard on yourself. Accept that you cannot possibly fix everything, and that is okay. Just continue trying to help others in realistic, tangible ways.

5. Don't Take Things Too Personally

You are vulnerable to criticism, and you see it as a personal attack against you. Do not. Understand that constructive feedback is meant to help you improve and better yourself. It is not a personal affront against your beliefs and values, but a tool to help you accomplish tasks more efficiently. Try to think about it objectively, from a purely critical standpoint.

6. Put Yourself First

You are selfless to a fault. Often, you forgo your own needs in order to take care of the needs of others. Although this is an admirable quality, it can work against you when taken to the extreme. This can cause you to forget about your health and well-being. Remember that to be able to help others, you have to help yourself first.

7. Be More Assertive

As an INFP, you are naturally quiet and reserved. Add that to your dislike of conflict, and you can sometimes allow yourself to be overlooked or taken for granted by other people. Although it can be difficult for a peace-seeking introvert like you, understand that most people are not aware of how you feel unless you vocalize it. The next time you feel uncomfortable about something that someone says or does, let them know.

The 10 Most Influential INFPs We Can Learn From

INFPs are intelligent and gifted people with a great capacity for empathy and compassion. When they apply these qualities, INFPs are capable of remarkable things. Here are a few influential INFPs who you can emulate and learn from.

1. Antoine de Saint-Exupery

Antoine de Saint-Exupery was a French writer who is best known as the author of *The Little Prince*, a poetic narrative which includes watercolor illustrations that Antoine de Saint-Exupery drew himself. Although the book looks like a children's book, it is actually a deep and insightful tale that makes profound observations about life and the world we live in. Antoine de Saint-Exupery is a great example of an INFP who used his creativity and artistic abilities to create something that has touched the lives of people worldwide.

2. Bill Watterson

Bill Watterson is an American cartoonist who is best known for creating the comic strip Calvin and Hobbes. Bill Watterson began drawing and making up stories in his head at a very early age, and like a true INFP, he spent hours thinking about the fictional world he had created. He also used his comic strips as a form of self-expression. However, he disliked the fame and lack of privacy that came with it.

3. J.R.R. Tolkien

J.R.R. Tolkien was an English poet and author who is most famous for creating the high fantasy works *The Lord of the Rings* and *The Hobbit*. INFPs are known for their vivid imaginations, so it is no surprise that J.R.R. Tolkien was able to create such a vast and profound fictional world, with fully-developed characters and backstories. He even created his own language! J.R.R. Tolkien is an excellent example of what an INFP can achieve if given the opportunity to explore the fruits of their imagination.

4. Edgar Allan Poe

Edgar Allan Poe was an American poet, author, and literary critic. He is best known for his poems and short stories, such as "The Tell-Tale Heart," "The Raven," "The Cask of Amontillado," and "Annabelle Lee." He became famous for his distinct writing style, which leaned toward the macabre. Although he achieved success as a writer, he was tormented by emotional struggles which continued until his death.

5. Vincent van Gogh

Vincent van Gogh was a Dutch painter famous for his bold and honest works of art. His art has inspired people all over the world and has influenced the way people see and appreciate art in general. He lived a misunderstood life and struggled with emotional instability and mental issues.

6. Hans Christian Andersen

Hans Christian Andersen was a Danish author who is best known for his short stories and fairytales. He wrote some of the most famous fairy tales in the world, such as "The Little Mermaid", "The Ugly Duckling", and "The Emperor's New Clothes." Hans Christian Andersen is another great example of an INFP whose limitless imagination changed the lives of people worldwide.

7. William Shakespeare

William Shakespeare needs no introduction. He is responsible for some of the most famous plays and poems in existence. In most circles, he is even regarded as the greatest writer the world has ever known. His works have been translated into almost all languages.

8. George R.R. Martin

George R.R. Martin is another writer on this list of influential INFPs. He is an American author who is best known for his series of epic fantasy novels, *A Song of Ice and Fire*. His books have been turned into the television series *A Game of Thrones*. True to his INFP nature, he has been quoted as saying, "In my imagination, I can come up with anything that I want. I can make things very large and very colorful."

9. Tim Burton

Tim Burton is an American director, writer, and producer who is best known for his gothic and macabre film style. Some of his works include *The Corpse Bride*, *The Nightmare Before Christmas*, and *Sleepy Hollow*. It is interesting to note that one of Tim Burton's closest friends, Johnny Depp, is also an INFP.

10. Johnny Depp

Johnny Depp is an award-winning American actor who has starred in numerous films. He is often seen portraying quirky and unconventional characters. In fact, according to him, he identifies with the lost-soul quality that most of his characters have.

Conclusion

As an INFP, you have many admirable qualities and natural gifts. You are intelligent, creative, and compassionate. You are driven by a strong set of personal values and beliefs, and you strive to heal the troubles that other people suffer from. You see the world as a kind and beautiful place, and you see the best qualities in other people as well. Although you are quite difficult to get to know right away, you are a loyal and passionate person who values the relationships you create with other people. This combination of characteristics gives you everything you need to achieve great things, as proven by other INFPs just like you.

However, some of these qualities can become liabilities when taken to the extreme. Your extreme selflessness can cause you to neglect your own needs. Your extreme idealism can set you up for disappointment. You also tend to be too hard on yourself when things do not go the way that you expected. That said, there are many ways to overcome these weaknesses and become a better, more successful person.

Choosing the right career is especially important for an INFP like you. Look for jobs that allow you to exercise your intelligent mind and artistic abilities, while contributing to the betterment of society and other people's lives. When it comes to relationships, remember that the people you love are human beings who are bound to make mistakes. That is okay. No one is perfect, and that only makes life more interesting and worthwhile.

Everything that you have read so far can help guide you toward personal development and a greater understanding of your purpose and place in the world.

Final Word/About the Author

I was born and raised in Norwalk, Connecticut. Growing up, I could often be found spending afternoons reading in the local public library about management techniques and leadership styles, along with overall outlooks towards life. It was from spending those afternoons reading about how others have led productive lives that I was inspired to start studying patterns of human behavior and self-improvement. Usually I write works around sports to learn more about influential athletes in the hopes that from my writing, you the reader can walk away inspired to put in an equal if not greater amount of hard work and perseverance to pursue your goals. However, I began writing about psychology topics such as the Myers Brigg Type Indicator so that I could help others better understand why they act and think the way they do and how to build on their strengths while also identifying their weaknesses. If you enjoyed

INFP: Understanding & Relating with the Healer please leave a review! Also, you can read more of my works on *ISFJs, ESFJs, ESTJs, How to be Witty, How to be Likeable, How to be Creative, Bargain Shopping, Productivity Hacks, Morning Meditation, Becoming a Father,* and *33 Life Lessons: Success Principles, Career Advice & Habits of Successful People* in the Kindle Store.

Like what you read?

If you love books on life, basketball, or productivity, check out my website at claytongeoffreys.com to join my exclusive list where I let you know about my latest books. Aside from being the first to hear about my latest releases, you can also download a free copy of *33 Life Lessons: Success Principles, Career Advice & Habits of Successful People*. See you there!

Printed in Great Britain
by Amazon